LET'S FIND WEDGES

by Wiley Blevins

WHAT IS THIN ON ONE END AND WIDER AT THE OTHER END?

A wedge! It's a simple machine. It can cut things. Chop! It can break things apart. It can hold things in place too.

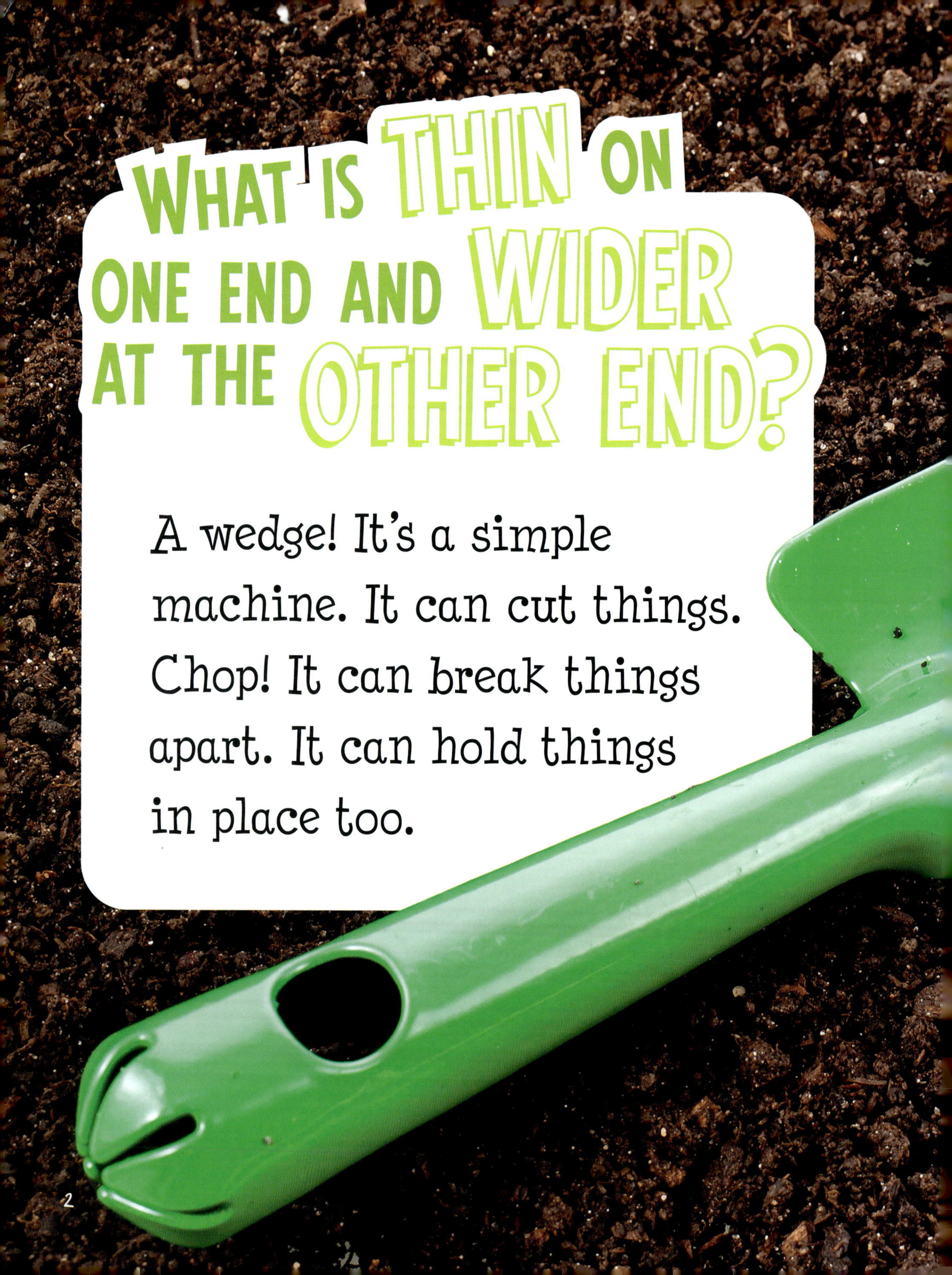

Where can you find wedges? You don't have to look too far. They are all around us!

LOOK IN THE MIRROR.

What can you see? You can see a whole set of wedges. They're smiling back at you. They're your teeth.

CHOMP! CHOMP!
THEY HELP TO BREAK APART YOUR FOOD.

A man needs wood for a fire. He grabs an axe. It is a metal wedge.

CHOP! CHOP!
STACK THE LOGS.

HOW ELSE CAN YOU STAY WARM?

Zip! Zip up your coat and keep out the cold.

A ZIP USES WEDGES TO OPEN AND CLOSE.

BACK AND FORTH.
BACK AND FORTH.

Have you seen this wedge at work?

A SAW IS A WEDGE THAT CUTS WOOD.

HOW CAN YOU KEEP A DOOR OPEN?

Push a wedge under it. That's all you do!

NOW THE DOOR WON'T MOVE.

A TRAIN'S POINTY NOSE IS A WEDGE.

It CUTS THROUGH THE AIR AS THE TRAIN SPEEDS DOWN THE TRACK.

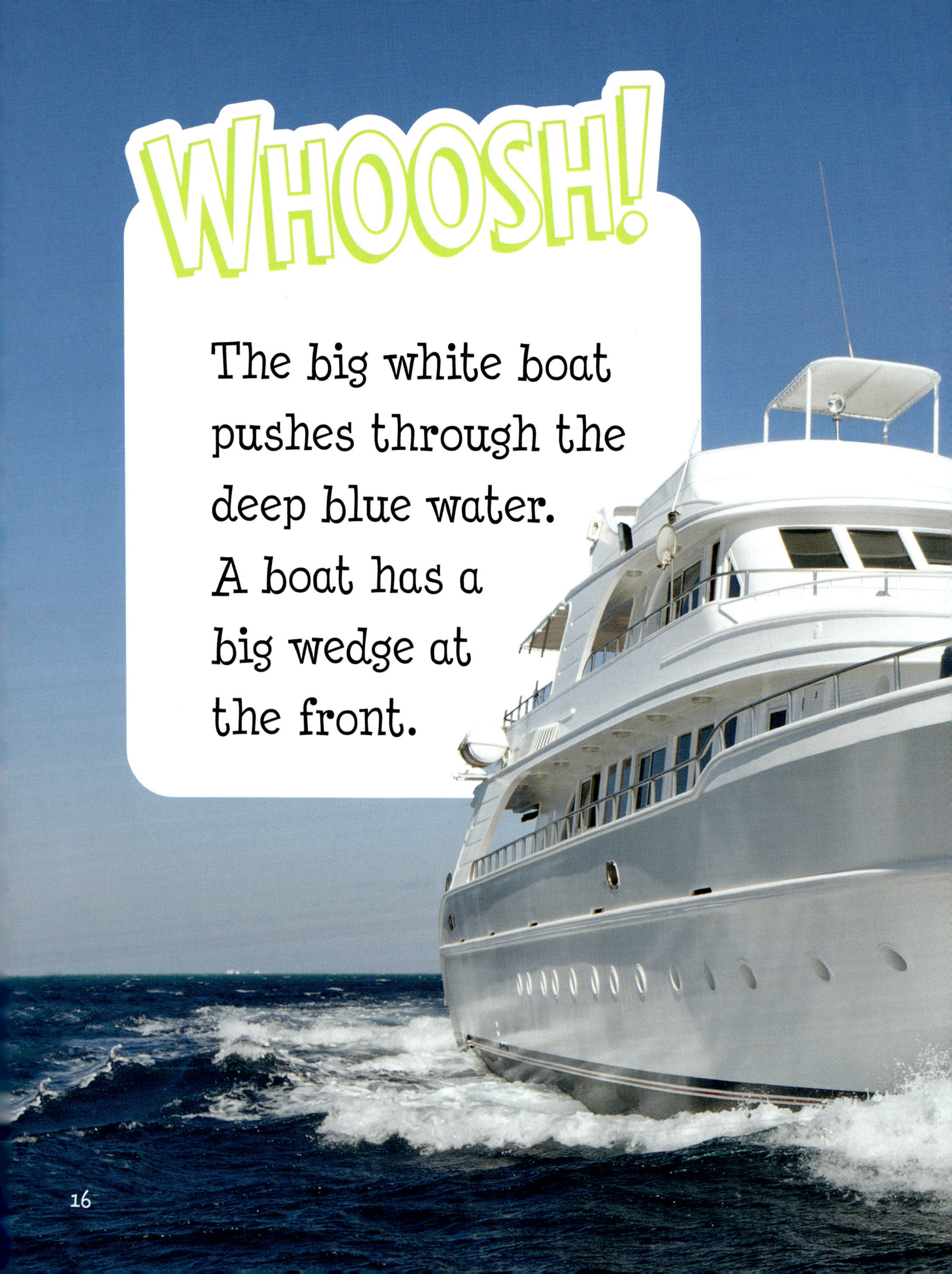

WHOOSH!

The big white boat pushes through the deep blue water. A boat has a big wedge at the front.

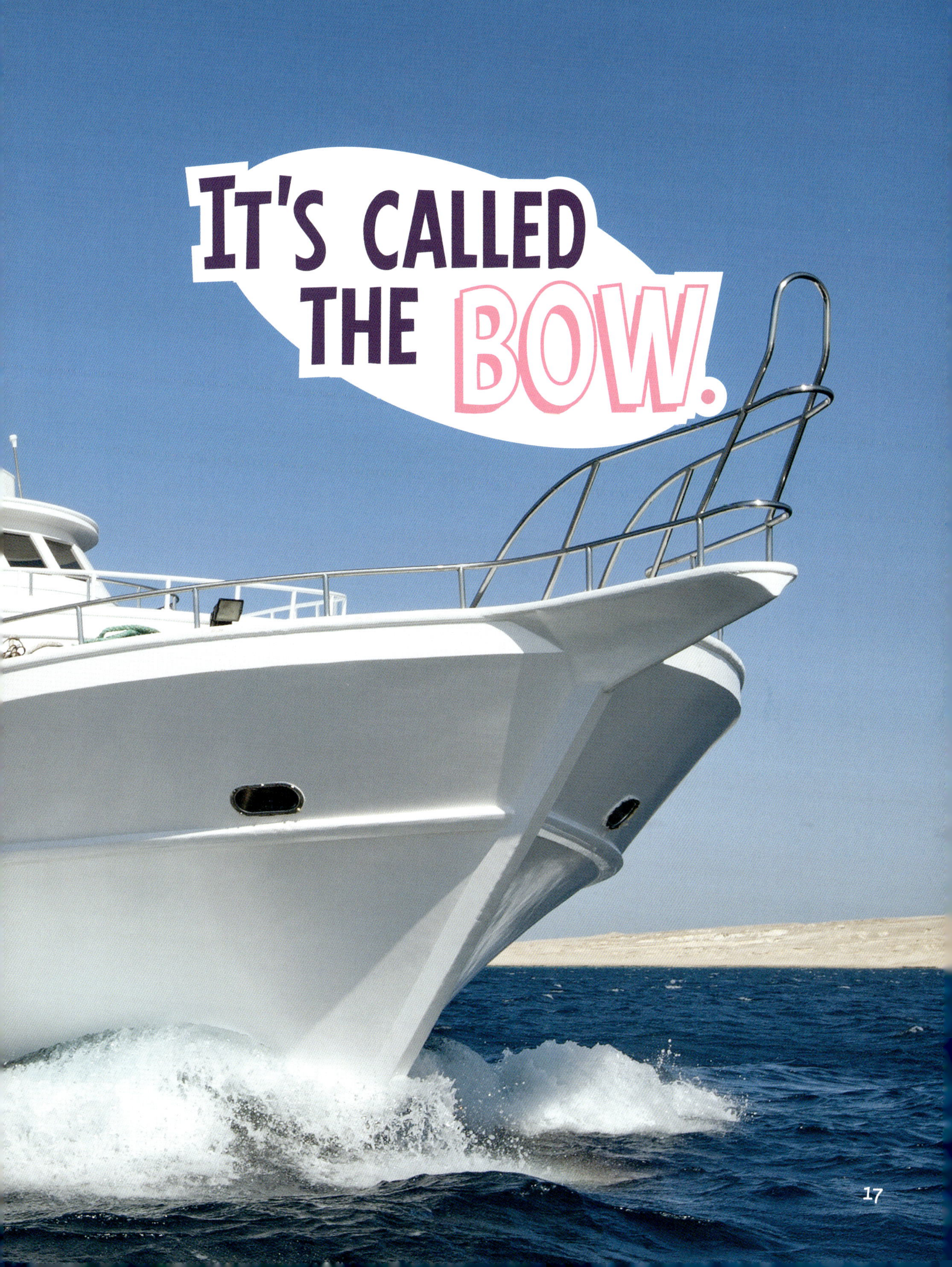
IT'S CALLED
THE BOW.

It's TIME FOR LUNCH.

Let's make a salad. A knife is a sharp wedge that cuts vegetables into small pieces.

CHOP!

HOW DO YOU CUT PAPER?

You need scissors! Squeeze the handles. Two wedges work together. **CUT!**

NOW
YOU HAVE PRETTY
PAPER HEARTS.

You need to dig in the soil. How? Use a spade. The bottom is a metal wedge. It breaks through the ground.

DIG SOME HOLES.
THEN WATCH
YOUR PLANTS
GROW!

HERE IS A SPECIAL NOTE.

A pin holds it up.
A pin has a sharp
point. It is a wedge.

It **BREAKS** THROUGH PAPER TO KEEP IT ON THE BOARD.

GOOD
WORK!!!...

BANG! BANG!

Hit the nail with a hammer. The nail is a wedge.

It PUSHES THROUGH THE WOOD TO HOLD TWO PIECES TOGETHER.

A needle is a wedge that pushes through fabric. Sew pieces together with a needle and thread.

boat bow
teeth
scissors
saw
pin
needle
knife

nail
spade
doorstop
zip
axe
train nose

Raintree is an imprint of Capstone Global Library Limited, a company incorporated in England and Wales having its registered office at 264 Banbury Road, Oxford, OX2 7DY – Registered company number: 6695582

www.raintree.co.uk
myorders@raintree.co.uk

Copyright © Capstone Global Library Limited 2022

The moral rights of the proprietor have been asserted. All rights reserved. No part of this publication may be reproduced in any form or by any means (including photocopying or storing it in any medium by electronic means and whether or not transiently or incidentally to some other use of this publication) without the written permission of the copyright owner, except in accordance with the provisions of the Copyright, Designs and Patents Act 1988 or under the terms of a licence issued by the Copyright Licensing Agency, 5th Floor, Shackleton House, 4 Battle Bridge Lane, London, SE1 2HX (www.cla.co.uk). Applications for the copyright owner's written permission should be addressed to the publisher.

ISBN 978 1 3982 0505 5 (hardback)
ISBN 978 1 3982 0506 2 (paperback)

Edited by Erika Shores
Designed by Kyle Grenz
Media Researcher: Tracy Cummins
Production by Spencer Rosio
Originated by Capstone Global Library Ltd
Printed and bound in India

Image Credits
iStockphoto: emholk, 22–23, malerapaso, 30 middle right, Marilyn Nieves, 8–9, robcruse, 12–13; Shutterstock: aapsky, 31 bottom right, Andrey Eremin, 30 middle left, Atstock Productions, 26–27, Butterfly Hunter, 30 top middle, Dragon Images, 20–21, Fast flash, 30 bottom right, Gecko Studio, 30 top right, Hurst Photo, 31 middle left, junpinzon, 24–25, KK Tan, 4–5, Kozak Sergii, Cover, Louella938, 31 middle right, Madlen, 2–3, Matveev Aleksandr, 30 top left, MrVander, Design Element, Nikita Rublev, 31 bottom left, Olivkairishka, 6–7, Ortodox, 14–15, Paul Vinten, 16–17, Phoderstock, 10–11, Shift Drive, 18–19, Tatyana Vyc, 28–29, trekandshoot, 31 top left, Vadym Zaitsev, 31 top right, You Touch Pix of EuToch, 30 bottom left

British Library Cataloguing in Publication Data
A full catalogue record for this book is available from the British Library.

FIND OUT MORE ABOUT SIMPLE MACHINES BY CHECKING OUT THE WHOLE SERIES!

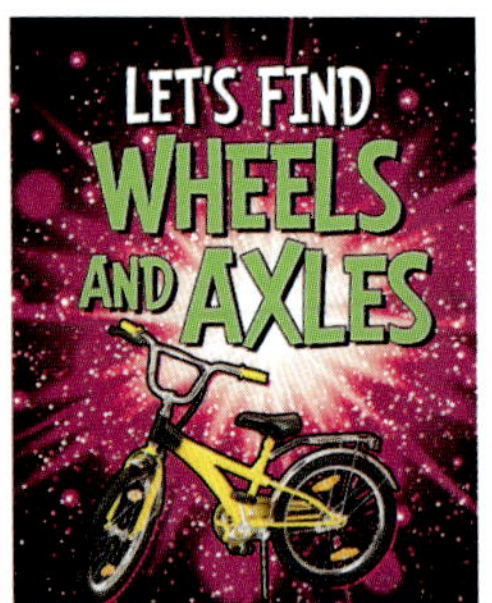